CW01512169

ASK FOR
WHAT
YOU
WANT

Owning the Art of Inquiry to
Get the Most Out of Life

ASK FOR
WHAT
YOU
WANT

Owning the Art of Inquiry to
Get the Most Out of Life

CLARA ANGELINA
DIAZ-ANDERSON

EXTREME OVERFLOW PUBLISHING

Dacula, Georgia

Extreme Overflow Publishing

A Brand of Extreme Overflow Enterprises, Inc.

P.O. Box 1811

Dacula, GA 30019

www.extremeoverflow.com

Copyright © 2024 Clara Angelina Diaz-Anderson. All rights reserved.

No part of this book may be reproduced or transmitted in any form or by any means electronic or mechanical photocopying, recording or by any information storage and retrieval system without the prior written permission of the author, except for the inclusion of brief quotations in critical reviews and certain other noncommercial uses permitted by copyright law.

Published by Extreme Overflow Publishing

Printed in the United States of America

Library of Congress Catalog in-Publication

Data is available for this title

For permission requests, contact the publisher.

Send feedback to info@extremeoverflow.com

This book is dedicated to my beautiful family, Alex, Angelina, and Christopher. May you always remember to ask for what you want.

TABLE OF CONTENTS

This book follows the Clarifying Transformation Methodology, which I developed and use with our clients, as well as in our coach certification programs. This model introduces a new concept and demonstrates its application in real-life scenarios. By sharing stories and examples, we prepare you to practice what you have learned and observe how this newfound wisdom supports your desired outcomes. The model begins with "Asking for What You Want," using The 3 C's of Clarifying: Clarity, Courage, and Conviction. For permissions to use this model or to become a certified professional coach, please visit www.clarafying.com

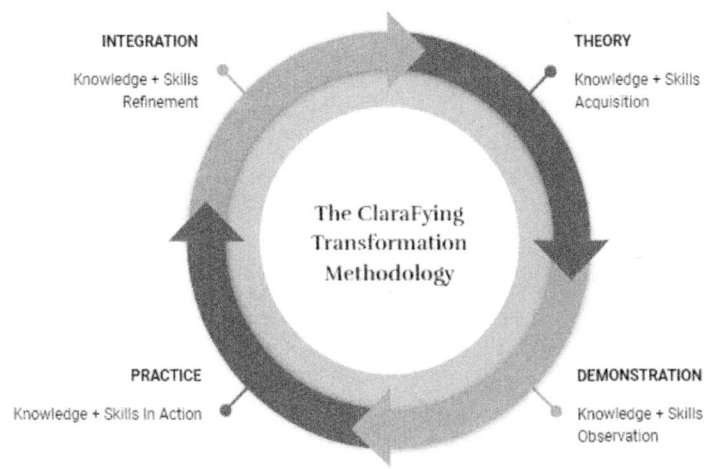

Figure 1. The Clarifying Transformation Methodology

ASK FOR WHAT YOU WANT

INTRODUCTION

The warm water massaged my tired face as an insight of deep realization came over me in that one place where all amazing ideas come forward for me, the shower. I was thinking about the impact that I want to make with this book, the legacy that I want to leave behind for my children and humanity. Deep down in our hearts, we have the desire and the ability for more. We can awaken that power by daring to ask for what we want in life, love, work, joy, you name it! And the women and men who know that, there is more available and dare to ask for it.

If society teaches us to raise obedient children, failing to encourage the questioning of systems of authority, how can a person grow up to be a confident conscious leader if they are not allowed to inquire and ask questions? How can we develop children and adults to ultimately ask for what they want and at times demand it?

And that's when the message of this book became crystal clear to me.

My goal is to remind every person reading this book of the truth — that we are co-creators of our reality. That when we are in our truest essence — living in the freedom to question, inquire, request, and create, we are utterly free.

The recognition of this power can open the door for you to make significant and even transformational changes in your life.

You get to choose to use this creative power to change not just yourself, but the world, for good. And the access to the knowledge that allows you to become a conscious leader, **starts by learning to ask questions, inquire, go deeper** and to take yourself so seriously that you ask yourself, people and the universe what you really want, so that you can live out the answers to your wildest dreams and see your request fulfilled and questions answered.

Ever since I was a little girl, I always loved to ask questions. Some of the questions I remember asking were, why is that so? And why is this so unfair? I asked a lot of why questions and got a lot of short answers as a result. And maybe, not the right answers. The adults around me sometimes were not able to answer my questions, or didn't have the emotional capacity or time to engage in my incessant inquiry. I grew up believing that asking too many questions was a way of troubling people and shaking up the status quo; another form of causing trouble. It wasn't until I went through a process of changing that belief in myself, that I began to fulfill my purpose in life — to accept my purpose and be an agent of positive change.

In this book I use the words: **ask, inquire, inquiry and request** interchangeably. In my work as a coach and teacher helping leaders become more authentic, confident and effective, the tool I use the most in coaching and teaching is inquiry, also known as socratic questioning. Inquiry is simply asking questions for the purpose of discovering new information. Socratic questioning, born from the philosopher Socrates, who developed this method of teaching, is asking questions for the purpose of students finding the answers to the deepest questions inside of themselves.

This book will give an introduction to the power of questions and awaken in you the desire to use your "Requests Muscle." At the end of each chapter I will give you an inquiry to exercise your request muscle. Let me give you an example of how this works. I'd like to start by sharing a story of how owning the art of inquiry can change your life like it did mine.

One cloudy afternoon during the fall of 2019 I was driving to run a workshop for senior citizens based on my 1st book *Create Your Best Year*. It was one of those days where I needed an extra dose of motivation because it was cold, rainy, and gray outside. As the island gal that I am, this is not my favorite kind of weather to go outside in. It was fair to say I was a little out of it that day and that caused me to miss my usual exit to get to my destination. I ended up taking a right turn into none other than the campus of Harvard Business School (HBS). I had never been to this school before and had no idea that I was driving across the famous HBS until I saw a building with the big Harvard Business School edged into the top entrance of one of the century old buildings. Once I realized where I was, I dared to ask the question that has changed my professional life since that moment.

How can I teach here one day? I wonder, what would need to happen in order for me to work here one day? My mind paused in wonder and then the voice of doubt took over. Saying things like, but you don't have a PhD, you don't want to go back to school do you? Or the silliest one was, Do they even hire Dominican women? Let that silly idea go, I said to the mean chick in my mind. And I did just that. I posed the question and before my mind gave me more reasons to stop asking and dreaming I decided to focus on getting to my destination which was only two minutes away from the campus. Fast forward to four months later and I get an email from a friend about an opportunity to facilitate and coach in a class called, Interpersonal Dynamics Lab at none other then, yup you guessed it, Harvard Business School. There I had the opportunity to teach, facilitate and coach my own cohort of thirty 1st year MBA's along with thirty other colleagues and combined we support 938 students to develop more empathy, increase their listening skills and exercise the interpersonal skills necessary to create long term mutually beneficial relationships.

I share this story because I dared to ask the universe and even myself, what would it take for me to work here? And the universe responded in the form of an opportunity. This is one of the many of examples you will read about in this book.

The book *Ask and Its Given* by Jerry and Esther Hicks, says that, "when you ask, the universe immediately responds." Our job is to release the resistance that keeps us from making or receiving our request.

In my example, it was my very own thoughts that called in a powerful possibility and wanted to take the question out of my mind. The authors continue on to say, if you are anything like me, when doubt creeps in, you may tend to sabotage yourself and do something to prove yourself right. In my case, I decided to release the resistance by asking the question and then letting it go.

When the time came for me to interview for the role at HBS, I was scared. I asked myself this question: What would I have my clients or my best friend do in this situation? I would tell them to bring their full selves to the interview, listen, ask questions, have fun, and don't be shy to let them know how much you want this opportunity. And so my friends, that is just what I did. And was hired on the spot.

I share this story because I want you to bring forward your wildest dreams and start inquiring within yourself.

What do *you want* now?

_____

_____

Start developing the Clarity, Courage, and Conviction to work on your receptivity, capacity, and confidence to allow the answers to be revealed to you.

The power of inquiry allows us to create change by discovering more, having more information to work with, allowing us to make better decisions, and supporting ourselves and others to evolve. In a time where the world is so separated, where we are at times at war with ourselves and even each other, it is still in our ability to inquire, be still, and reflect with ourselves and with each other in a way that will allows us to take actions that will liberate us all, allow us to evolve and change into who and how we're meant to be.

I believe that we are all children of God, the source of the universe, a higher power, that with infinite intelligence has orchestrated and brought us into being. It is in this recognition that I invite you to explore the questions below and get intimate with yourself.

Who you are?

Explore how do you identify, what are your character traits, what do you enjoy, what stage of life are you in? Where are your greatest strengths and how are you contributing those strengths in your profession? Fall in love with learning about how your identity contributes to the way you interact with the world. When you start to see yourself as an infinite and free spirit who is choosing to be on earth and support others in awakening to their power, everything will change for you.

Expand your identity beyond what others have said about you or what you have believed about yourself up to this point.

What are you?

You are a star (literally, you are made up of the same stuff of stars; water and carbon in the same proportions to that of the earth). Essentially we can say that you are a star on earth. Even our limbs represent the 5 pointed star. These two pieces of information alone, tell you that there is a supreme intelligence that is responsible for you being here. Make a list of all of your personal and professional titles. Mother, father, son, friend, cousin, aunty, uncle, neighbor, brother, sister, and ask how can enjoy these relationships or come up with your questions about what you want and what you want to give in this relationship. Watch the magic unfold when you ask questions like, How am I loved in this relationship? How do I love?

Whose are you?

No one is an island? We all belong to various communities and play different roles. This defines who we are. For example, I am my employee's boss, my daughter's mother, my husband's wife, my mother's daughter, my sister's sister and so on. When we choose to see our connection to a greater whole, it allows us to re-energize our purpose, knowing that who and what we are affects the greater communities that we are connected to. It also invites us to inquire more and deeply in your own life. The people around you, your community and the world at large needs you and everything you bring to that role, desperately.

In this book, I invite you to awaken the power within, be a positive agent of change, a better leader, and liberate yourself and others through the power of inquiry. I invite you also to give yourself and others permission to maximize their time on this earth or specifically in any role, by using the power of inquiry in your every day life.

I want you to really consider how your cultural upbringing (culture being a set of adopted ideas, customs, behaviors of a group of people) has shaped your ability to inquire or to not ask questions or to ask for more or to not ask for things at all. How has your culture and the way that you have been raised shaped you up to this point? I also want you to consider the types of questions you ask and what happened when you asked these questions and in what settings.

And lastly, I invite you to practice and to build a community of support around you. Once you start inquiring, you are going to awaken, change and expand your life as well as those around you. As you do, liberate yourself from the limiting beliefs and patterns that have kept you from moving forward in any area of your personal and professional life. Free yourself from the idea that you need to work harder, that the world is hopeless, that people don't change, that you can't change, that you don't deserve a better environment, settling for ok, that you are too busy to work on yourself, that you are too old or young to make significant changes in your life, that you don't have impact and that you can't contribute to a better world. Free yourself from anything that holds you back from believing that you can ask for what you want and deserve to receive it!

CHAPTER 1

Learning To Ask
For What You Want

"You get in life what you have
the courage to ask for."

-Oprah Winfrey

H uman beings are born with a natural ability to ask for what they want and need.

Look at a newborn baby who hasn't even learned to utter its first words but knows exactly how to inquire about what it needs through a cry or many other signs.

Socialization takes place in us all sometimes to the extent that we now become so hesitant to ask for what we want that we silently abuse ourselves because we dare not speak up for ourselves.

When Kim, a 35-year-old, Haitian-American, single mother of a teenage boy and Senior Director of Clinical Operations at a major hospital in Massachusetts, came to work with me because she felt burnt out from the way she was being discriminated and overlooked for promotions by her male boss, we got to work right away.

One of the first inquiry and request experiments we set out to work on was for her to use her "Requests Muscle" and inquire about taking a week off at the end of each month because she has so much vacation time accumulated. No one had ever done that before, but Kim knew she needed to advocate and give herself time to heal from the burnout, devise a strategy, and adopt a new work pace. After some resistance from her boss and HR, through the power of inquiry, she got what she needed and then went on to find a new position where she was in a healthier work environment, with an extra $50,000 added to her salary.

Learning to ask for what you want is not always easy

when you have been conditioned by outside influences to believe that it is "bad" to do so. Asking for what you want can be the difference between life and death. Having had the courage to learn to ask for what you want requires you to consider eight things: know what you want, understand what your motivations are, be specific, consider time and place, and practice active listening. Let's explore each of these principles.

1. **Know what you want.** Take the time to reflect on what it is that you really desire. Ask yourself, "What is it that I want?" "What do I desire?" "What are my goals?" Learning to differentiate each, giving meaning to the ones you want, the ones of others, or the ones that you think you should have. To learn to ask for what you want, we have to get clear on defining what it is that we want. And own that clarity.

2. **Understand what your motivations are.** You have to be able to ask yourself, why you want what you want. Get clear on exactly why so you can get to the core

of your worthiness. I also believe that when you're clear about what you want, the way to get what you want becomes more apparent.

3. **Learn to be specific.** To be specific is to also give yourself full permission to envision in full color. See exactly what your desire is going to look like when it comes to fruition.

4. **Consider the environment, choosing the right time and place.** Timing and context matter. At the moment you ask, we want to make sure that we are priming the environment so that what we ask for, we can get. This has so much to do with knowing how to choose the right time and place and picking the moment when you think the other person is most receptive and when they will be minimally distracted. Then, you can base your request on having a higher chance of actually receiving what you're asking for or getting the yes that you want.

5. **Use assertive communication.** When you're using assertive communication, it means you are being clear, direct, and confident in expressing your needs and your desires, avoiding passive or aggressive, language, and using positive language that allows the other person to be receptive to what you're asking.

6. **Practicing active listening.** Active listening is the ability to be able to listen to what is being said and clearly rephrase or paraphrase what was said. Understand the feeling of what was communicated so that you can adjust according to the needs of the conversation.

7. **Listen carefully.** After you make your request, listen to other people's responses carefully, and be open to feedback. Acknowledge their perspective and be open to negotiating or compromising if necessary, and not give up at the sign of resistance. Listening carefully will also help you be better prepared to position how you ask for what you want.

8. **Be prepared for different outcomes.** Sometimes we make a request asking for something and instead of getting exactly what you want, you get something else. It kind of opens up a whole other set of options. When you ask a question, you make a request and are opening yourself up to receiving what you want, sure, but you're also opening yourself up to different experiences.

Learning to ask for what you want is not always easy, but as you will grow to learn, it is very well worth it.

Time to practice strengthening your Request Muscle.

Strengthen Your

Request Muscle

—— Exercise ——

EXERCISE #1:

- Put pen to paper
- Set a time for 12 minutes on your phone
- Spend 12 minutes writing down the answer to this question:

What do I want the most in life, that I don't already have?

Do your best to write this on paper and for the next three days notice how glimpses of what you want start to appear.

_____

_____

_____

_____

_____

_____

In addition to the Clarafying Transformation Methodology, this chapter will introduce our Ripples of Influence Model. In this model, our clients are invited to think about the impact that they can have on the world at large. Behind this theory is a knowing of our conscious power, the impact we have on others and the connection to the larger systems of life.

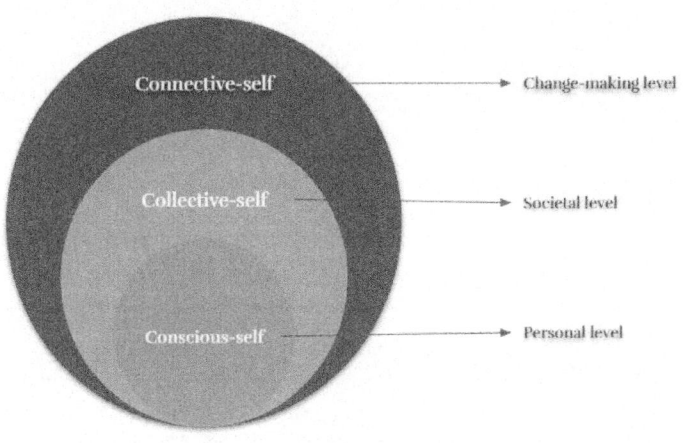

Figure 2. Ripples of Influence Model

CHAPTER 2

Lack of Awareness

"Let us not look back in anger, nor forward in
fear, but around in awareness."

- James Thurber

My executive coaching partner, which is
what I called client Emanuel, Senior
Manager at a major philanthropic
foundation, 42 years old, married father
of two, wanted a promotion, like yesterday. He felt that a
year of poor performance during the 2020 pandemic
had set him back in his professional trajectory. He
wanted to be seen as a trusted advisor and he needed
more income with his new baby coming. We got to work
right away. His first inquiry was, how can I share the
impact of my work with the top decision-makers in the

organization? How can they become advocates for my advancement?

Emanuel was promoted to Director of one of the biggest social change programs and received a $50,000 raise, all because he dared to ask and navigate the conversation. In gratitude and disbelief, he would repeat to me, "Clara, I was not aware that I could ask for that."

When we think of having awareness around being able to inquire, we can go in many different directions. There are even times when we can be open to different levels of awareness.

Many of my clients have told me time and time again that they were not aware they could ask for something, inquire, or investigate what they wanted. They were used to just taking what was before them and forced to do something better with it; sometimes without really getting to the root of why they were settling in the first place.

Think about this like you would a baby. When we see babies, we see that they want to be aware of everything. Babies are not inherently aware of the world around them. You can always see them looking around curiously. That is the same curiosity we need to have when it comes to inquiring about how to live the life we want. It makes me wonder, when does that awareness and curiosity leave us?

Having a lack of awareness of something really calls us to think about the speed of our lives. Our level of awareness and our ability to look, notice, and wonder is directly proportional to the speed at which we live our lives. Overthinking, an output of a lack of awareness, is like traveling at a fast speed in a car. You will see everything and won't really notice anything. You're not really aware of what's around you. The same concept applies to life. Sometimes seeing the path you are forging ahead can be missed along with the importance of everything you are driving by. However, when you drive through life at a slower pace, you can actually look at what's around you, what's available, notice, and wonder. This is where inquiry can come in.

In wonderment, many of my clients have told me that they wish they knew how to slow down like they know now because in the now, they have a bigger awareness of the various ways they can inquire by asking questions, investigating, and opening themselves up to what is really in front of them. What life is really presenting them — everything they want.

This is especially true for people of color who have been trained to live in survival mode, moving at a fast pace for so long. For many, it is what society expects. It's what we have all been socialized to define as productivity. And it is often in this space that we are not aware of the fact that we can slow our pace and ask for more of ourselves and of others.

As leaders, we can ask for more out of situations. Being trained to have all of the answers, to be the expert in something can come as a double-edged sword. One human being cannot possibly know all things about anything. A lack of awareness of this principle can be a huge setback, and an even bigger problem because you will only make decisions from a limited perspective and with limited information.

As a leader, there is a special call to be aware of and mindful of symbiotic relationships; a mutually beneficial and supportive relationship with your direct reports. And with the people that support you. These relationships work as a safe space where you can ask them, what they think, what they would do in a situation, and when appropriate, you can create a space where you can inquire about the type of support you need from them. Understand that you don't have to have all the answers alone.

There are different levels of awareness that I like to refer to as the Phases of Awareness. These phases are cultivated through a cycle of intention, choice, and noticing. The different phases of self-awareness are:

- Phase 1 Having self-awareness.

- Phase 2 Outer noticing.

- Phase 3 Communicate what you notice. And lastly,

- Phase 4 Cultivation.

Phase 1: Having Self Awareness

When you have self-awareness, you are able to more deeply notice how you feel, what you need, what your gifts and talents are, what your limitations are, and where you want to actively grow. Having self-awareness is having an intimate relationship with yourself, fully noticing and knowing who you are. Self is the heart, body, mind, and soul. Having self-awareness is a lifelong endeavor and a well-worthy one. When you have self-awareness, you will have a deeper capacity to be aware of what's going on around you.

Phase 2: Outer Noticing

When you have the awareness of outer knowledge, you have a deeper ability to notice details. While self-awareness develops patience, slowing down enables your ability to notice, the little things. Like the sparkle in someone's eye or a birthmark on their face that you didn't notice before. You may notice the way that your employee lights up when she speaks about a certain project or when she speaks about her daughter. This outer noticing allows you to see the energy of your team shift when you choose to include everyone or when you don't notice how good your team member feels when you acknowledge their efforts in a team meeting. Or when you ask them questions instead of telling them, or when you take the time to coach instead of lecture. When you embody this outer noticing you cultivate it through intention; intentionally committing to be more aware every day. Take time to do your mindfulness practices and anything else that helps you to slow down and make informed choices based on what you notice. Those choices won't be beneficial to you only but they are going to be beneficial to the larger group, your community, the people that work with you, and those who you consider your family.

Phase 3: Communicating what you notice

Once you're making these different choices. It's important to communicate what you notice and what you're choosing to do differently. You can start by communicating with yourself, and then communicating with the important people around you, who support you in your everyday life, both personally and professionally.

Phase 4: Cultivating Awareness

Give yourself time to cultivate awareness. Many of my clients who come to me are going in to work on their days off, even working on their birthdays. Now, if that's your personal choice, that's one thing and is your choice. However, always putting yourself last and putting work first is not sustainable. And if you're reading this, you know exactly how this feels.

A key marker of cultivating awareness is not being fully aware of your gifts, talents, and the ways that you can cultivate your own genius in the world. Like, knowing what your value really is to a company. And on an even bigger scale, what is your value in the marketplace?

The question to ask when you are here is: Am I being underpaid? Or, am I being properly compensated? To develop awareness around what you can inquire about at work is to do the work of asking:

- What do I need?
- What are my gifts?
- What are my talents?
- How is my role?
- What is the value of my role in this company?
- What is the value of my skills and talents in the marketplace at large?

Then, you can develop an awareness around the compensation that comes with communicating that value properly.

Perhaps you just became aware that your efforts had a great impact on the company. You might ask:

- What was your role in it and what was the outcome?
- How can you take what you have done, the impact you made, and communicate it in a way that shows your value?

Another point of cultivating awareness is to practice being aware of healthy ways to become successful. We have equated climbing up the corporate ladder with working more hours or doing more work when doing or giving more is not necessarily the way to get us more.

You may have bigger responsibilities and a bigger team, or even a bigger budget and bigger projects to manage. Still, that doesn't necessarily mean that your work hours need to double to get what you want. Inquire and actually explore the different ways of still getting to that new corporate position or being in that higher responsibility position without having to sacrifice your health and well-being.

Cultivate every opportunity by learning to also ask for help, without being afraid to ask for it. Also avoid not investing in valued relationships, because you feel the need to be doing everything on your own, especially for people of color, who believe you don't want to owe anybody any favors. This level of lack of awareness will not serve your highest good.

We forget about the value of interpersonal currency. Interpersonal currency is the trust that we build with people over time when we are just connecting with them and getting to know them on a human level, and not necessarily just to get them to do something for us. It's building those relationships and caring about people before you need them. When you ask for help and you're aware of who can help you within your organization, you'll also be aware of your role and value within the company and within the company's objectives, and can continuously seek clarity to provide the most effective contribution to the team. You also become aware of why you need to be successful, and what collaborators need from you as a part of that process.

Focussing on your soft skills and relationship building can be the greatest way to catapult your next career move. Stay aware of the needs that you have internally because showing up early and staying late with your head down won't produce the return on investment that you're looking for. All of these things lead to dissatisfaction, you leaving a job prematurely and really driving attrition.

When we can get ourselves and the people around us to develop awareness, we can inquire more of ourselves, of the environment we are in and allow this level of cultivation to influence our reality. Then, you can be clear on where you want to be, where you want to go in your career and be open to exploring alternatives in the workplace or in the marketplace.

By extension, cultivating awareness threads together with it the idea of having emotional intelligence. When you cultivate self-awareness you are aware of your emotions and you know how to manage them properly, to care for yourself, and to support those around you. A helpful practice is to document your achievements and your progress regularly. When you do, analyze them to promote your continued growth in up-leveling your awareness, skills, and your genius. Another practice is to stay educated and informed about your field, your career, and always seek ways to be a better player in your role learning to pause to figure it out.

Sometimes the alternative is to take a moment of pause. It's not as easy as it sounds to take a moment to pause. Literally, pause and breath. Then put pen to paper. Write about what you're going to do to start your day, or start a project, or start anything for that matter! Ask yourself, what is my intention? What exactly do I want to achieve and why? It's all your choice.

Choice is choosing exactly what you are going to do and determining how you will change your behaviors to align with helping you obtain what you desire to create, change, or influence. Choice is power. In this power, you want to continue doing what your soul is calling for - where you are actively repeating these steps throughout your life. Once you are clear on your intention, make the choice to take action. Taking action cultivates your awareness.

Cultivation is not a destination. This is about a journey. Cultivation is about expanding your ability to be intentional with your choices over and over again. This allows us to gain greater wisdom and an ability to exercise our inquiry and requests like a muscle. The more you inquire, the more information you're going to have and the higher chance you are going to have at making a difference in your life and the lives of others; the difference that you're here to make.

Prior to becoming a coach full time, I had a career as a Spanish interpreter, specifically, in the immigration field. I was so happy to have this job to finally be able to work in something that was natural to me, and to be paid so much to do what felt like such an important job. It was just mind-blowing. While I was extremely happy to have this job, I started to notice that the supervisor was micromanaging me. She would micromanage the way that I worked my interpreting assignments. I could choose if I wanted to work, either the morning court sessions or the evening, afternoons, or both. If I was finished, in five minutes, I was free to go, and I would still be paid for my whole morning with plenty of time to go about my business. So, I would strategically choose the days and the times that I wanted to work based on who the judge was, and what kind of docket they had that day.

Over a couple of years, I had it down to a science. There were weeks when I would only go into the courtroom, sign in, say a couple of words, and be free to go. I wouldn't work any more than like five hours a week. After some time, my supervisor started to notice that I would leave early a lot. She started asking me to come and check with her to see if I was needed anywhere else. As a good employee, I did. When I started to do that, I would then be put in, another case, which ended the glory of me being able to leave early and still get paid for my full day.

One day, I was walking in the hallway, about to leave and she knew I was ready to leave. She asked me if I wanted to make some extra money. That's when I started to question what was this really about. She said, Well, I have this case on the sixth floor with this other office you can go interpret. And you can get paid in cash. I was shocked when I realized that the reason why she couldn't keep putting me in these cases after I was finished was because she was pursuing another assignment so she could get paid double.

Here's the lesson, sometimes we are so grateful. We're happy to be doing our job and want to do a good job that we miss what else is going on.

After I was presented with this additional opportunity I realized how much I had been missing. It really had me go outside of my immediate world and think about what other places could I be interpreting. What other ways could I grow in my profession? I started to really understand my value in the market. As a result, I went from making the $40 an hour I was extremely happy about to making hundreds of dollars an hour interpreting privately. This would have never happened if I hadn't experienced a situation that could expose a full lack of awareness for my value, the opportunities that were all around me, and the different dynamics that were at play.

A lack of awareness around being able to inquire sets us back so much. As leaders there is so much more information available to us if we just ask. Your job is to create conditions where everyone can thrive. And everyone can help move the mission forward. Your job as a leader is to hold the vision and to stay aware of yourself, what's going on around you, and of the people that support the vision you're carrying forward. Your goal is to ensure that your impact is felt even in your absence. This is calling for leaders to become aware of the fact that there is a dormant power that we all have that awakens in asking the right kind of questions, investigating, and wanting to know the truth of things, in a way that is not just the norm, but is actually celebrated.

A lack of awareness of anything really keeps us from our true evolution as human beings and as leaders. I inspire you to ignite a desire to be more awake and present in whatever you're doing. Look around and feel free to ask questions, investigate, figure out what's best for you, and have full awareness of what's possible and what's available. Start to grow your awareness, really notice and wonder about things in your life, things in your community, in your workplace, and in the world so that you can start to inquire about and possibly, and eventually make a difference.

Strengthen Your Request Muscle

Exercise

Exercise #2:

- Put pen to paper
- Set a time for 12 minutes on your phone
- Spend 12 minutes writing down the answer to this question:

What qualities am I aware of in myself and those around me that can support me in preparing to receive what I want the most?

Do your best to write this on paper and for the next three days notice how glimpses of what you want start to appear.

_____

_____

ASK FOR WHAT YOU WANT

CHAPTER 3

Advice Giving

"Never take the advice of someone who has
not had your kind of trouble."

- Sidney J Harris

We love giving advice and most of us don't take the advice. When was the last time you followed advice without feeling like that advice in some way validated an idea that was already your own?

Advice-giving is one of the most difficult obstacles for leaders to overcome. As leaders we have gained so much knowledge and even wisdom from overcoming challenges over the years that we want to help others avoid the mistakes and lessons learned along the way. While there is always a time and a place to offer our expert guidance, we have to remember that the job of a good leader is to create more leaders; not just by imparting knowledge and giving guidance but also by coaching and development.

As a leader, creating an environment for inquiry, is to be able to create environments and situations where other people can discover answers for themselves.

I teach a class called Leadership Coaching Strategies and Executive Coaching Mastery at Harvard University. And I've often found myself echoing, "No advice-giving, do not give advice!" Through this class, students come from all over the world. On an average, seven to eight countries are represented at any one time ready to learn how to coach and use coaching to really help them enhance their leadership skills, and their abilities to create conditions where other people can thrive, and they can positively influence others.

As a Coach of Coaches, I use this principle in my

business as well. In my coaching structure, we found ourselves changing the practice from, "Go ahead and practice the skills that we have been teaching you" to just "practicing inquiry." We saw that advice was just the thing that people went to for comfort. I got really curious and started to ask why this was the case. Essentially, what we were seeing was advice-giving, as a form of an obstacle to actually listening.

Interestingly enough, I started my career in coaching and mentorship wanting to help other people as a self-proclaimed advice giver. I loved giving advice. Once I learned and started to really get deep into the skill of coaching, it showed me that people already have inside of them what they need. There are things of course, that as experts, we make suggestions for and advocate for but they have to be okay with that.

Giving advice from the place of, you're an expert, and you have so much lived experience, more than the other person, does not consider the fact that the person in front of you does also. Assuming that the person in front of you cannot come up with their own answers or assuming that perhaps they haven't tried the advice that you're going to give them, doesn't help.

Instead, we can employ a term that I use a lot with my students called, "Humble inquiry." Humble inquiry is the art of asking questions to answers that you don't know the answer to. Let's say someone is asking, "Tell me, how did the meeting go?" Instead, ask from a place of actually wanting to know, of being open and curious to what the person is going to say, without rehearsing in your mind what you already think they're going to say. When you feel the urge to give advice you want to keep in mind what your intent is. Is your intent really to be in connection and community with the person in front of you? Or do you want to give advice because you want to feel important or because you want to show how much you know?

At the heart of the matter, many of my clients, when

they are giving advice, instead of actually inquiring, they are already stating the answer because they feel compelled to help people from their sense of compassion, like it's their job to give advice. I ask them, but is it really your job to give advice? Or is it your job to help them produce results?

There's also this difference between what is solicited advice and unsolicited advice. Are you often the giver of advice solicited or unsolicited? Or are you at the receiving end? And how does that feel for you? As we are going on this journey of really owning inquiry, and being leaders who will create conditions and support and liberate others, we really need to stay aware of how much solicited or unsolicited advice we are giving. Think about how much we are talking and how that is affecting us.

In today's culture, where we are usually moving with a sense of urgency, and at the speed of light, we are called to become aware of our tendency to perhaps give advice and instead shift to more of an inquiry model of getting curious and asking questions. It requires a certain level of patience that many of us just don't have, for many, many reasons.

As leaders, let's start thinking about what questions we can ask ourselves to be put in the position of being mindful, and patient to see others in a positive regard, that does not need our advice.

Strengthen Your

Request Muscle

—— Exercise ——

Exercise #3:

- Put pen to paper
- Set a time for 12 minutes on your phone
- Spend 12 minutes writing down the answer to this question:

Did you take the advice? If not, what question could that person ask you that would have helped you come up with your answers?

Do your best to write this on paper and for the next three days notice how glimpses of what you want start to appear.

ASK FOR WHAT YOU WANT

This chapter will introduce our 7 Keys to Active Listening Skills Model. In this model, our clients are invited to work through the cycles of our conscious power to listen, hear and respond to the larger systems of life.

Figure 3. Active Listening Skills Model

CHAPTER 4

Fear of Inquiry

"The truth has nothing to fear from inquiry. Be wary of anyone who would discourage questions."

- Paul John Moscatello

Why are people afraid of inquiring?
Why are people afraid to ask for what they want?

The first reason is because someone just doesn't really want to know the truth. Another is that they don't want to change.

Essentially, the fear of change, of things being different, can shake the current reality. Regardless of whether the reality is desirable, or not desirable, they're just afraid of change.

I was recently with a friend who took me to a day spa as a gift for my birthday. My friend, from the Dominican Republic like me, is an attorney and a mother of two. We were having a conversation about, where we are in this stage of our lives and how we feel more comfortable with really expressing our truth and expressing what we want, and really putting effort towards getting the things that we that we truly desire. Not what others want for us, or what society is expecting but what brings us joy. She mentioned that she was looking at properties on the oceanfront of the Dominican Republic, close to a place that she had previously spent in an Airbnb.

"You know, they are actually selling property there," she told me.

"Oh, really?" I said, "Okay, well, did you ask how much it cost?"

"You know, I didn't," she responded.

And it wasn't a matter of whether she could afford it. It was the idea of allowing herself to dream to the fullest, feeling free to inquire about the details of what she wanted.

Having what you want is not just a belief that you can have it but rather the confidence in seeing yourself have it. And it's not about if you're going to have it, it's when. It's getting past that point of thinking that you are worthy. That is not even a question anymore. The answer to whether you can have what you want is in your environment.

In the wrong environment, you can be afraid of:

- not asking the right way.
- not receiving the answer.
- what the actual answer is.
- the information that we may uncover that is going to cause us to lose control of the present.

Apart from looking at your environment, you must be willing to change by being open to new information. For leaders, sometimes we get into positions of leadership based on what we've known or what we've done up to that point. However, the mark of an exceptional leader is to employ humble inquiry and to allow him or herself to be influenced by what they uncover. Letting go of this fear of inquiry, is to make a decision ahead of time to look at our blind spots and potentially make a new decision based on what we find.

President Franklin D. Roosevelt, said it best, "The only thing that we have to fear is fear itself." As we continue exploring this theme, the teacher in me wants you to know exactly what fear is so let me break this concept down. Fear is a psychological belief of expected or unexpected pain or threat upon a person. It is also the unpleasant and often strong emotion that is caused by the same anticipation, awareness, or danger of what comes with physical changes, increased heart rate, increased blood pressure, and cortisol levels that really drive up your anxiety.

As we are owning our ability to inquire, to lead with consciousness with compassion to help liberate others, we become aware of the fear we have often referred to as inquiry, anxiety, or just simply a fear of asking questions and seeking answers. Inquiry is the ability to pose questions and seek answers for the purposes of learning, discovering, and supporting another in achieving a unified goal. It is the psychological condition that many of our fears can manifest in so many different ways; in the workplace, classroom, social settings, and in intimate settings, as well. As a leader, it's important to be aware that many people have this fear within them already. If this is happening in your environment, one of the things that can come to light is appearing ignorant, or in other words, looking stupid.

One of my clients Rita, 44, a Boston public school teacher said to me, "You know, I really didn't want to ask questions at work, because I felt like they were gonna say, 'Oh, she's supposed to know that.'" Fear of appearing ignorant or like you don't know your job can really set you back because your focus is limited to the negative possibilities.

But, if you're willing to ask questions, especially at

work, we need to find our allies. If you're concerned that asking questions is going to make you look unintelligent, or uninformed in front of others, I want you to think about the fact that many other people feel the same. Studies have shown that people in a workplace environment are afraid to ask questions because they don't want to seem stupid, or appear ignorant. So, if everyone else is feeling that way, you're not the only one. You can be the brave person who gets an answer for everyone.

We decided to survey more of our clients on this topic of fear. Another big fear that we found when we were interviewing people was a fear of judgment; being afraid of what others are going to think or perceive of you because you're asking this question. This category of people are afraid of the judgment criticism, ridicule, or being made fun of in a moment of inquiry. The beauty is in the fact that just asking a simple question can lead to really shaking up the culture or the status quo; the way something has been done. One of the antidotes to overcoming this type of fear is to continue to tell yourself that what happened in the past is not happening in the present. Doing so can really help you to reprogram your mind to be more courageous and more confident in your ability to ask and in your capacity to receive the answer.

It is your human right to be able to ask and seek answers, which doesn't always mean that you're always going to find the answers. Nor does it mean that your question is going to get the response or is even going to be acknowledged. There is no guarantee of any of that. But it is your right to be able to ask and seek.

As we interviewed other clients, we found that fear of rejection, in that their questions were going to be completely dismissed. Or that they will be seen as a bother for seeking information. I remember talking to a fellow teacher, she was a preschool teacher. She told me about a time when the director of the school asked all of the teachers to come to an open house. So she asked if they were going to be paid overtime because it was beyond her regular working hours. Her boss responded with yelling and said that anyone who didn't show up to the open house would be fired. On top of that, the director continued to say that this was an unpaid responsibility that they had to fulfill. The teacher decided that she wasn't going to go because she wasn't getting paid. She was suspended for two weeks from work by her boss. In her circumstance, her retribution for posing a question that challenged the status quo came at a cost. When you're posing a question of this nature, consider what your relationship with the person is and evaluate how much trust is in this relationship. Also, consider what your intention is when asking your question which will help you to avoid this fear or to prepare for unfavorable recourse.

The other fear that we found from our client survey is fear of drawing attention. One of my executive clients told me a story of how she sat in an executive meeting and asked a question about a business process that she thought could be done more efficiently. Her goal was to galvanize the efforts of everyone in the room, but instead ended up being tasked with taking on the project because she raised the question. I've seen this happen to so many people in Corporate America where people feel that if I open the can of worms to ask, I might be tasked with an extra project. In the end, so many have just gone with the flow because most people don't want more work.

Overcoming fears involves building confidence and self-assurance. On a personal level, being able to build confidence and self-assurance comes through practice. Practice asking more questions and if you feel the fear, practice asking through it. The more you do it, the easier it gets. Also, you want to be in an environment or help to create an environment where inquiry is not just tolerated but is welcomed and celebrated. If you can't influence your environment and put yourself in an environment that welcomes inquiry, open dialogue, and communication, seek guidance from a coach, therapist or counselor to help you address managing fear, if it significantly affects your daily life and your work.

To be an effective conscious leader who leads without fear, do this internal work of having positive self talk that actualizes the inner courage to ask posed questions and seek answers when needed.

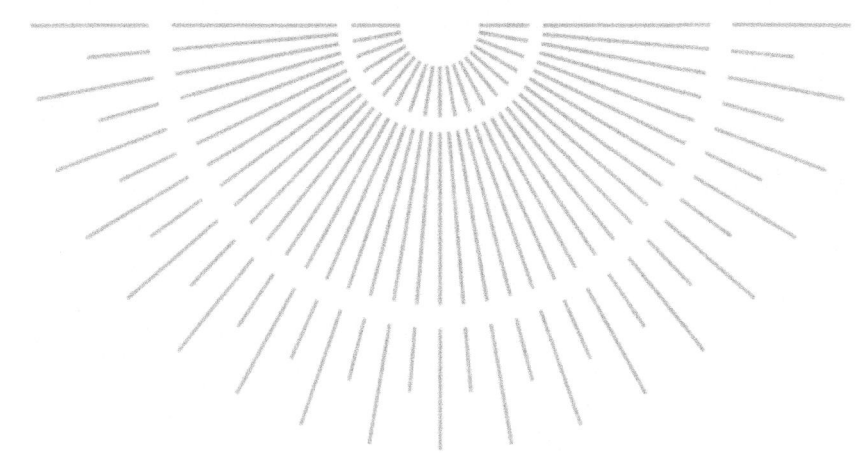

Strengthen Your Request Muscle

Exercise

EXERCISE #4:

- Put pen to paper
- Set a time for 12 minutes on your phone
- Spend 12 minutes writing down the answer to this question:

What am I most afraid to ask for in my personal life? What am I most afraid to ask for in my professional life?

Do your best to write this on paper and for the next three days notice how glimpses of what you want start to appear.

_____

_____

CHAPTER 5

Cultural Influence

"A people without the knowledge of their
past history, origin and culture is like a tree
without roots."

- Marcus Garvey

O n a beautiful summer day, specifically on a Friday, I was having a celebratory lunch with one of my dearest clients. When I asked her what she felt was the most valuable piece of our coaching relationship? She said, our coaching helped her grow a muscle that she didn't think she needed to grow. When I asked her what that muscle was, she said, "It was the muscle of being bold, being able to ask for what I want, give myself permission to go after what I want, and to open myself up to possibilities to step outside of my comfort zone." When I think about all of those things that she mentioned, it boils down to confidence.

Confidence is being in the psychological state of believing that no matter what you face, you are going to be able to handle it. Truly believing that you have the ability, and the capability of being able to face whatever comes at you is a power. And it got me thinking because I didn't expect that to be her answer. I expected her to tell me more concrete things that she'd gained from our coaching, like the promotion that she had just received where she received a 150% increase in her salary. She's now making well over the $200,000 mark, in the healthcare industry. The jump from manager to director that she has now made is amazing! I thought she was going to tell me about that, not about this muscle. Her testimonial of what was most valuable to her, this muscle she grew that she didn't expect to grow, really got me thinking a lot about what point in life has us forget this muscle of confidence. Where does the difficulty to ask for what we want, to inquire, to make requests really come from?

I have another client who has also been working on getting a raise, not necessarily a position change, but a raise. She already was making six figures, well over $100,000. When I gave her specific instructions to use a technique of paraphrasing and asking questions, until she left the room with the answer that she wanted or the answer that she needed. She couldn't do it. She was being left in the dark by her boss constantly telling her that, "I'm gonna get to it. I'm gonna look into it." But there was never a concrete response as to why, when or where she was gonna get her raise. When I asked her why she hadn't said anything, she told me that asking was aggressive to her. She said she didn't want to be aggressive. In return, I asked her what was aggressive about asking. She said, "Well, I know that I'm speaking from my trauma from living and growing up in a Caribbean household where I was not allowed to really ask for the things that I wanted. It wasn't that I was told that I couldn't ask, it was just that culturally, I looked at my environment, and I knew better not to ask. I knew that we didn't have the money for those things."

In this client's case, it wasn't necessarily that her parents told her that she couldn't ask for things. It was that she recreated the environment that told her she shouldn't. And so now that she's an adult, she's still struggling with this idea of not feeling like she should ask for what she wants, which might come off as offensive. In many cases, early childhood experiences affect the degree of our capacity to give ourselves permission to inquire, request from others, or request something for ourselves because we have been programmed to do otherwise.

The culture that we grow up in completely influences the way we think and the way we see the world. It influences our relationship to access. Not being able to inquire takes away the right to be curious, the right to learn, even from a young age. As a parent, I know that the more curious my children are, and I love that they're curious, the more work it is for me. Sometimes, I don't have the capacity to provide them with all the answers to everything that they're requesting, everything that they are inquiring about. But I give the best answers I possibly can which in some cases means I send them to inquire on their own. With this client sitting in front of me, I thought of how I could inspire her to explore life through questions on her own.

As we peeled back the layers, I asked her to consider what her degree of belief was. Meaning when you desire something, that you may not have today or tomorrow, how willing are you to take the necessary steps to achieve it? Do you believe enough in an abundant universe working in orchestration for what you desire? Then, from a scale of 1 to 100, where would you rate yourself on taking that action?

I have coached many clients who are still learning to embrace living this way which has so much to do with their perception of what is available to them and how that perception was established. Now, think about when you were first understanding. As small children, we cried, we got our milk, we knew how to get our needs met.

Once we learned how to communicate the same, we were trusted to learn that you are not always going to get what you're asking for all the time. At the same time, this same rearing teaches us to negate our own needs and wants, and desires. Even in a conversation, wanting to ask for more information about something, we feel like we shouldn't. Yet, this is your right to be curious. It's almost as if you're penalizing yourself when you're not allowing yourself to naturally ask questions at a turn or out of place. It literally debilitates your life creating a negative life experience and then being let down. It enforces these feelings of lack within you. This belief that you're not going to get what you want, says, why ask in the first place?

Even bigger than these internal feelings is the overall culture of white supremacy we live in. It's this air of perfectionism that we breathe as a socially acceptable norm. And if you're not meeting those norms, you're labeled as less than. Then as less than, you believe you are also unworthy of asking or of receiving things that you want. It's the not asking that keeps us from being our true selves, whole, strong, amazing, and fully believing in the idea that you can ask and have whatever you want. As we live in a culture that unfortunately marginalizes certain groups, people of color, or other differences unacceptable to mainstream beliefs, we become the role models. We can also look around and find role models that either reinforce our inability or make us want more.

Explore what the role models are in your life. What were the role models around you that helped you to want to have conversations about growth transformation, and enlightenment?

I have gone on a journey of discovery and developing awareness in a culture and environment that has shaped who I am and have shaped my values.

This is an opportunity for you to look at your inner child.

What's your environment telling you to ask?

What does internalized oppression really look like in yourself, if that exists?

Who are the people around you who uphold limiting beliefs or beliefs of limitlessness? Of possibility, of transformation, of change, of newness of evolution?

We're constantly changing and evolving, and that is the truth. Anything other than that is, dying. You want to move forward. You want to take what has strengthened you from your culture and adopt new ways of being that support you need.

This moment is an opportunity and a call to take a moment to take a pen and paper and write down what you value most. Answer, what are maybe three things that you value the most, other than money?

Allow those values to set the trajectory for your goals, your short-term, your long-term goals, and to drive your daily behaviors and naturally motivate you to inquire about what will help you, your community, the people around you, and the world at large. Live from a place of values on purpose to live intentionally and live for the greater good of all.

Culture is like a flowing stream. If we are fish that don't realize our true power against the current of trends, expectations, and society we can never truly evolve. Take this opportunity to examine those cultural influences in your life.

STRENGTHEN YOUR

REQUEST MUSCLE

—— EXERCISE ——

EXERCISE #5:

- Put pen to paper
- Set a time for 12 minutes on your phone
- Spend 12 minutes writing down the answer to this question:

What were the gifts your culture of origin gave to help you make the most of life? What are the gifts your current cultural environment gives to support you in maximizing your life?

Do your best to write this on paper and for the next three days notice how glimpses of what you want start to appear.

_____

_____

_____

_____

_____

_____

_____

_____

_____

_____

_____

_____

_____

_____

_____

_____

_____

_____

_____

_____

_____

_____

_____

_____

_____

_____

_____

_____

_____

_____

_____

_____

_____

_____

_____

_____

CHAPTER 6

The Power of Questions

"Only the one who does not question is safe
from making a mistake."

– Albert Einstein

Have you ever noticed a toddler, when they want something? They ask and ask until they get it. I live with one, so I am speaking from first-hand experience here. There is a lot we can learn from children before they are socialized and from good parenting as a leadership position. But what stops leaders from asking more questions?

One of the things that stops leaders from asking more questions is not knowing what kind of questions to ask. In order to get better at asking questions, we simply need to ask more questions.

Questions literally send you on a quest. When you ask a question, you are opening up. You are opening up the space for new information to come in. A study done by Harvard business professors Holocene Woodworks and John called it, the surprising power of questions. They found that questioning within organizations is a powerful tool that unlocks a couple of different values and gems within the organizations. It spurs learning and the exchange of ideas. It fuels innovation in performance improvement, builds rapport and trust among team members, and can mitigate business risk by uncovering unforeseen pitfalls and hazards. It creates a culture, in an organization, a community in a home, and a safe space in any form of environment, where people can exchange ideas, fuel innovation, and improve performance like they feel like they belong to. They trust each other, simply because they are able to ask better questions. And so why is it exactly what we should consider when asking questions?

One of the first benefits of asking more questions is

the ability that it has to naturally improve our emotional intelligence. The more emotional intelligence you have, the more you learn how your emotions can be used to drive results of your objectives. The better question asker you become, the more emotional intelligence you have, the better at questioning you become, its a cycle. When we look at pieces of behavioral science we learn how to better frame questions, and choose answers that can influence the outcome of the conversation. Drawing the maximum possible positive result from every interaction.

Another to consider is the idea of giving ourselves permission to ask more questions. Socrates believed that people have the answers to all the questions that they have, within them but they have to ask the right question in order to unlock that answer. Having this vast idea and creating a school where people can really think and philosophize asking big questions within the sphere of coaching, therapy, and all forms of professions that require being a good questioner has stemmed from this idea of the Socratic method. The Socratic method essentially, is being able to ask questions in such a way that they elicit a deep response from your conversation partner. In other words, ask more questions so that you can warm up what's called a request muscle. We all have this muscle within us. We also have to think about the tone in which we're asking questions, the sequence of when we're asking questions, and the purpose of why we're asking a question. It becomes then, really important to think, again, about the type of question, the tone of the question, the sequence in which you're, you're also framing the framing of the question also matters.

The thing is that most people, they just don't understand that asking more questions, creates an environment in which people can ask more questions. It actually drives learning and innovation. It has been found through research to really improve interpersonal bonding. In a study done at Harvard Business School, students were given questions. Two groups of students were given two different sets of questions to ask; one with the experiment of interacting with a low number of questions and the other group with a high number of questions. The group with the higher amount of questions walked away feeling profoundly closer and more heard than the group that was given the instructions to ask less questions. Proving that the more questions we ask people, the closer it brings us in relationship and community.

The type of question that you want to ask really depends on the best approach for any given situation, the goals of the person asking the questions, as well as the goal of your conversation partner. From there, we can consider two things, does this conversation need to go even deeper and is this a cooperative conversation, or a competitive conversation?

When we think of a cooperative conversation, we're talking about the kinds of conversations that are about building relationships and working together in collaboration?

It's about working together to accomplish something together. A competitive conversation is one where it's about uncovering information, sensitive information that perhaps you don't want to reveal or information that you're being questioned on that can have a potential risk if you were to reveal the information. Essentially, in a competitive conversation, two people are trying to uncover information that will serve their own interests.

People don't know what to ask, because there are times when we think that we have to have the right answers and the right questions in our minds ahead of the conversation. The good news is that there is something that we can do. There is a type of question that we can always lean on. And that is, follow-up questions. Every time someone asks a question, you can choose to respond and ask a follow-up question based on the response. Your follow-up question can birth an emergence of new content or a new turn in the conversation.

When we determine a conversation to be competitive right away, we really want to try to ask tough questions first. Why? Because research has shown that people will be more willing to open up if we ask tough questions from the beginning. Of course, the sequence of your questions really depends on the circumstance. At the end of the day, the goal is to build a relationship, before asking tough questions. There are four types of questions that are a part of what I call the conversational intelligence network.

1. Intro questions.

You can start your engaging questions with intro questions, such as, "How are you?" or "Where you're from?" Those kinds of questions don't have a lot of weight or risks.

2. Mirror questions.

Next, there are mirror questions. These kinds of questions are literally mirroring back to someone what they have just said to you. By being able to mirror back really helps someone feel heard.

3. Switch questions

Then we have questions I like to call full switch questions. These are questions that can change the theme completely all.

4. Discovery and innovation questions

Discovery questions are questions that challenge assumptions. Challenges then go deeper into looking at different situations. They can help exchange feelings and implications of what issues concern you what or exploring what can be done to build trust in this situation? Discovery questions also include sharing facts and experiences, ideas and explorations. Exploring desires and describing success as well as defining what would give us the feeling that we were successful. They also include a level of Innovation that can really help generate bountiful possibilities.

Using this network of questioning increases oxytocin, deepens connection between people, creates perspective shifting, and thought provoking idea development.

The Socratic questioning Socrates came up with six, six types of Socratic questions that I teach my students in my coaching certification. They are:

- conceptual clarification questions,
- probing questions,
- probing rational reasons and evidence,
- questioning viewpoints and perspectives,
- probing implications and consequences and
- questions about the question.

Conceptual clarification question ask why and What does this mean?

- **A probing question** asks to verify or disprove an assumption. It asks what else can we be assuming?

- **A Probing rational reasons and evidence question** asks why is that happening? And asks for an example. It may further ask questions like: What is the nature of this? How can we be sure of what you're saying?

- **Questions of viewpoints and perspectives**, asks how can we look at situations in a different way?

- **Probing implications and consequences** asks, "then, what?" kind of questions. It explores what would happen after something happens? And what are the consequences of such an assumption?

- **Questions about questions**, asks questions you don't choose to answer. Meaning when someone asks you a question, you would respond with another question like, "what does this mean?" It is a pause in thought about the response you are willing to give because if you're opening up the space for questions, people can also ask you questions in return. And so it's important to remember to make sure to determine ahead of time, what the intention of the conversation is. And, what kind of information you want to share or what kind of information do you want to keep to yourself ahead of time, so you can decide what you want to share and what you want to hold private?

In a recent class I've taught at Harvard, specifically, the class that I was teaching in this time was leadership coaching strategies. In every class, we do a demonstration. We have a student who graciously volunteered and had 25 minutes to be coached. Her question was about how could she be successful in her new role. She had just left a previous organization and was now at a Vice President at a university.

In the twenty-five minutes that I had with her, I spent twenty of those minutes asking questions. Employing what call "positive inquiry." I didn't know the answers or the context of her situation before our coaching session. But by the end, I asked her the one question that changed her life forever. I asked her to identify for herself right now, the one thing that she needed to do in order to be successful in her role?

As my student sat with that question she went back to her role as Vice President at a university and really started to see a lot of changes. Big shifts happened between her and interactions with her direct reports. She saw that she was getting quicker results, with people being more responsive in getting things she asked to be done. Ever since our session, she has been asking more questions, giving space for people to respond and that alone has made such a big difference. As you are reading this, I would say as Einstein says, question everything.

The same Einstein theory says that if I had an hour to solve a problem, and my life depended on it, I would spend fifty-five minutes thinking of the right questions to ask because if I knew the right questions, I would be able to solve the problem in five minutes.

We all want solutions. One of the ways to reach

those solutions is to question everything. And to do it from a place of curiosity, wonder, positivity, humility, and with a solutions-focused lens. The power to ask more questions opens the door for you to make the most out of your life, your year, month, day, relationships, role, whatever you name it. Ask for what you want.

STRENGTHEN YOUR REQUEST MUSCLE

—— EXERCISE ——

EXERCISE #6:

- Put pen to paper
- Set a time for 12 minutes on your phone
- Spend 12 minutes writing down the answer to this question:

What do I want for myself today? What do I want for my loved ones? What do I want for work partners? What do I want for my community? What do I want for the world?

Do your best to write this on paper and for the next three days notice how glimpses of what you want start to appear.

_____

_____

_____

_____

_____

_____

_____

_____

_____

_____

_____

_____

_____

_____

_____

_____

_____

DIAZ-ANDERSON

125

Not so final words

Claudia was one of my very first coaching clients who was just 28 years old when she arrived to the United States from Colombia.

She came here by herself but had a best friend already living here in the United States. Her best friend helped her to gather the money to get the plane ticket to come. Like many immigrants and many people who want to create a better life for themselves, they scrape all the resources they have and decide to go on a quest to answer the questions that are burning inside of them. That question is usually around discovering if there is something better for me out there. The answer to this for her and all of us is a resounding, yes!

As we've uncovered throughout this book, sometimes we are not aware that we have the power, the ability or even dare I say, the permission to question, to inquire on the journey that we have been on so far. I have shared with you stories of my clients who have dared to question and inquire about whether there more. To question, how can I get to the next level? What does it take? Who can help me?

I believe that every leader, every person, every human being wants to awaken the leader within them. To do so, every leader needs to be able to honestly sit and answer the questions: Who am I? What am I here for? Who can, how can I get to the business of doing what I'm here for?

This includes identifying who can help you in this process of inquiry. Sit down and answer those questions for yourself. When you do, you start to stir up the dormant leader within. Or if you are already awakened as a leader, you will be empowered by the strength of your inner leader to stand up even straighter and make an even greater impact.

There's no better investment than the one you make into really getting to know you.

What if I told you that a year from now, just like my client from Colombia, you too could achieve her dream of getting her master's degree and doing the work of media production and television editing in an impactful way? She managed to get her Masters's degree, find her dream job, and create for herself those opportunities that allowed her to fulfill her purpose in what she came to the United States to do, which was to, in her words, to have a better life.

We all want some version of that, not just for ourselves, but if you're reading this, but for the opportunity to serve a lot more people. Remember to have the courage, to ask the questions, to inquire, to investigate, to go deeper, because you're worth it. It's part of the formula of learning to own the art of inquiry. This courage is also necessary for us to consider who we are in relation to the people around us, to the people who raised us, and to the programming that has brought us up to this point.

It's very important to be able to ask yourself the question of what is mine and determine what are you carrying from the people you consider family, as well as from the community from where you draw strength. There will be positive and negative things that you uncover about their influence. However, we draw strength from knowing our individuality coupled with everything that has shaped us to this point. There is strength in acknowledging that being able to make a decision and say, from this moment forward, I am going to start to make an intentional decision to take action that will bring me one step closer to living the life I want, can change the trajectory of your life forever.

One step at a time going as slow or as fast as you'd like towards the things that are calling you, is the path that is calling you now. Answer the questions that are inside of you. Can I make more money? Can I study architecture? Why should I go into business? Should I go get a PhD? I want to live in front of the ocean. How can I start to do that? How can I start to make a bigger impact? How can I start to take better care of myself in the process? Then, ask even bigger questions like, how can I make the world a better place?

We make the world a better place when we take advantage of the moment and inquire, one question at a time. This is the time for us to awaken to our power and our ability to co-create through deeper inquiry. I urge you to join me on this quest. Together, we can awaken more leaders.

Thank you for taking the time to read this book.

About the Author's Journey:
Asking For What She Wants and How She Got Here

"You can be a conscious creator of your life
through a deep understanding and merging of
who you are, who you want to be, and
who you are called to become."

- Clara Angelina Diaz-Anderson

THE JOURNEY

I am Dominican. I was born and grew up in the Dominican Republic until the age of eight, where I went by the name Angelina. My Dominican nickname was "antenita de vinil," from the show El Chabo del 8, a vinyl antenna to be exact, because I was always so aware of my surroundings and what people around me were saying and doing. I think I was born with more of a heightened awareness than the average child. This severe case of hyper-vigilance would later become one of my superpowers: Claircognizance. This term describes a spiritual 6th sense defined by having a deep and almost instant knowledge about people, things, and situations. It goes beyond the apparent and available information to others. It's a profound intuition, usually accompanied by a physical gut sensation that what you perceive is true.

In my case it turns out that there can be spiritual benefits to a chaotic childhood, being born on a beautifully lush island, colonized by patriarchy, nurtured and fed by women who have traditional oppressive roles, and still manage to do everything with grace, beauty, and gratitude to God, first and foremost just the way they have been taught for generations. I now know that the pain of trauma can transform into heightened abilities that I have chosen to use for good.

Today, this heightened awareness is one of my superpowers as a social entrepreneur, executive leadership coach, and educator at Harvard University School of Professional Development and Executive Education. It has also supported me in creating my company, Clarafying Coaching and Consulting Institute, and as a published author of two books, Create Your Best Year (available in both English and Spanish) and my forthcoming book, will support heart-centered leaders to use their powers consciously, as systemic change makers and global citizens.

As a child, I constantly asked why everything felt so unfair. This level of inquiry brewed my determination to fix the blatant injustices I saw. I was naturally curious and highly observant of how people treated each other. For example, I noticed when the men in the house got the more significant piece of meat, leaving the children and women with the bonier portions. I also noticed that the women did more housework while the boys got to play more.

At the age of six, I remember making a promise to myself to live a different life from the unhealed family I was surrounded by. I was determined not to be a byproduct of my surroundings. At the time, I didn't know that all I was experiencing and witnessing would lead me to where I am today.

By paying attention to the things I didn't want, I could make conscious choices later on to avoid those things and instead embrace a new way forward, different from the environment I'd grown up in. I knew that I would not accept domestic violence at home, gender inequality, and blatant acceptance of ignorance and tradition. As a young girl, I observed the women in my life dealing with cheating partners, being solely responsible for the housework and child-rearing, all while being miserable and complaining constantly. I saw hopelessness in competent women who felt bound by these dynamics. I remember every single Saturday morning, instead of enjoying extracurricular activities, my siblings and would be forced by my father to stay home and deep clean the house simply because it was a custom and expected, although it was very inconvenient for the family. Cleaning can happen any day! I chose to break free from these unhealthy dynamics, seeking to cultivate a life of choice, equity, and freedom.

Overcoming the effects of living alongside poverty, domestic violence, chronic illness in my family, coupled with the hardships of migration, has made me tired of the way things have always been, stronger as a whole, humble and compassionate towards myself and others. I have learned to accept the parts of my past that caused me pain and transform that pain into fuel for my passion to help awaken others to their power in this life.

Growing up in the Dominican Republic, I grew up in two worlds: one of extreme poverty and making do with what you have and the other, having access and power. For me, it was a gift to be able to see both of these worlds. Both of my grandparents were entrepreneurs from my mother's side. My papa, Juan Antonio, whose nickname was Negro, sold eggs to local "colmados" (small stores). This venture was a family affair. I remember being part of the group encircling a big washing bucket where we repackaged the eggs for my grandfather's daily runs to sell to the local colmados. I loved helping out in this way; as a child, I thought it was the most incredible thing. I never thought of my family or myself as poor, but by definition, they were. Looking back, I didn't realize at the time how many people slept in my grandmother's house. We all shared a very small less than 1200 square feet. It was a small three-bedroom house, and often, 13 to 14 adults and children, were sleeping there.

On the other hand, my paternal grandfather was a successful business owner, shoemaker, and shoe designer with a big factory. He had many employees. One of my earliest memories with him was going to talk to each of his employees and asking them to make sure that they didn't waste my grandfather's materials and that they use his materials to the best of their ability.

Those early years before migrating to the United States with my parents and my three other siblings were a time when I learned about the dynamics of power, and financial freedom through entrepreneurship and envisioned a life bigger than what was presented to me.

THE LEARNINGS

I have faced many challenges on the road to becoming who I am today. Firstly, I learned that I had to be okay with being different from others around me. I can accept today that I'm not a bad person because I'm not always compliant with the status quo. While I used to feel ashamed at feeling different from my peers, I know now that standing out is one of my superpowers.

I also learned that I must care for my mental health continuously. I grew up in an environment of abuse and control, and it's important to me to break that cycle. Sometimes, these patterns are so hard-wired in us from an early age that we unconsciously create those environments in our adult lives as well, and I want better for my family. I show up with an open mind and heart, no matter what. As much as I humanly can, I am determined to provide my children with a better start so that they can go on to create healthy, fulfilling, and meaningful relationships.

I'll admit, I've been a lifelong people pleaser. I used to be the first to sacrifice my wants and needs for the sake of others. However, over the years, I've realized that I've twisted myself into knots and made myself miserable because of this programming of being an overover-givergiver y "siempre a la orden" — no, thank you! This is not a sustainable plan for me; sometimes, I am unavailable. It's called boundaries!

Today, I continuously make space for my joy and happiness!

A huge life lesson came from being an immigrant to the US and finding my place by learning a new language, adjusting to the culture, and feeling a sense of belonging in this country. I learned people live differently in the US than what I was used to. Closed doors versus open doors was so striking to me. I learned that if I can make it here, I can make it anywhere. It was ingrained in me that I had to work twice as hard as everyone else to get ahead, which is something I have had to deprogram in myself. I also had to learn English quickly to help myself and my parents as their interpreter.

I have also found that the US is not what people imagine it is from outside its borders. I have often found myself discouraged by the challenges of being a woman of color in a country where systemic racism is so prevalent. Then I am fueled with hope through my clients and students who, through their courage to lead, to be better and different, are helping to shape a better world.

I've made it my mission to support other rising leaders like myself "mi gente," to awaken their power of choice, their power to co-create and live the life that they imagine, not just for themselves, but also to create conditions for their families also to thrive, to heal generational patterns.

I have found over the years that one of my biggest hurdles is overcoming my own limiting beliefs. I choose now to meet these beliefs head-on, examine them, and toss them aside as much as possible. I refuse to be the person who keeps me small today. I lean into my power and my assets and I encourage myself to reach for the stars as often as possible.

An ongoing practice of self-compassion and self-acceptance has helped me overcome these challenges. I have sought the help of a therapist, coaches, spiritual guidance, and a lot of books. My educational path has been non-traditional. I had the opportunity to be homeschooled at a young age allowing me to learn to read by the age of three. I also spent a lot of time with my parents at work, setting me on a path of experiential learning. I have always loved learning my way, so when I learned that I could create my major at Lesley University, I did just that. I designed a major that allowed me to study what I loved: human potential and doing business for good.

Over time, I have learned and continue to remind myself that I don't have to do any of this alone and that having support is the best way forward for me.

I also experienced a near-death experience in the form of a car accident that felt like a reset in my life and transformed the way I saw myself and my purpose for living. I was driving to one of my many gigs at the time on a rainy day. My car hit a bump on the road and fishtailed, sending my first brand new car spinning into a guard rail that protected me from entering the Charles River across from the Harvard University dorms. As my car was spinning, I saw my entire life flash before my eyes like a movie. After reviewing my entire life in what felt like an hour but was only seconds, I felt an immense sense of peace come over me as I surrendered my life and asked God to allow my family to be okay with my absence. I closed my eyes and was surprised to find myself in my body without an injury. It felt like I was given a second chance to live life on purpose.

Many days, what keeps me going is the love of my community, my own family, my biological family, and my purpose to help others awaken and support me in living my truth every day.

I feel that my very birth was a disruption of the established norms and family system that I was born into. I was told that as a baby, my screams made the walls vibrate. My birth changed my family forever as I was my mother's first child and my father's first daughter. Today, I operate in spaces where I am the only woman of color or one of very few. My very existence in these professional spaces is a disruption of white supremacy and the status quo. I hope to continue using my voice to make walls vibrate, shatter glass ceilings, and shake the earth for positive change that ripples through all humanity.

THE INSPIRATION.

Growing up, I was inspired by the mysteries and magic of nature. As a child, I climbed trees and found a haven in them. I looked up at the vast expanse of the sky and was inspired by how expansive my life could be. I am still inspired by the sheer wonder of nature and all it gives us. I do my best to practice biomimicry, which is the science and art of emulating the processes of nature in all we do. One way that I learned to practice this is to remind myself that everything has its ebbs and flows — relationships, projects, and life in general — so I don't expect to be in perpetual harvest. There is a time to plant the seed, a time to water it, a time to watch it grow, a time to pluck the fruit, and then do it all over again.

I also learned that as a woman, I go through these stages of winter, spring, summer, and fall myself every month. As women, our energy levels fluctuate depending on the time of the month we are in. For example, our energy is low in our winter week (the week we are menstruating). We start feeling our energy return the following week as we enter the spring. Our energy peaks the following week in our summer week and starts to wane the following week in our fall week. Knowing this predictable energetic cycle allows me to plan my month to do my best work when I feel the most energy and to have absolute grace and care for myself in the weeks when energy is decreased. This has been so liberating for me and other women I coach because it has allowed us to be free of the idea that we must be on and perfectly producing 100 percent of the time.

Some of my biggest inspirations in my life have been the women who came before me. My mother Digna is a peaceful and gentle soul. I carry with me the legacy of my grandmother, Dolores whose resolve, generosity, and care for others inspire me to want to uplift all of humanity. My Godmother Ramona instilled in me the belief that I could become important and help others like her.

I often share about the power of the written word to inspire the world. I'm an avid reader and writer, and I've found that both of those hobbies expand my world and my thinking in ways that surprise me even to this day. I highly recommend reading about a variety of topics, as much as you can get your hands on. You will be on a grand adventure without leaving your couch.

I'd love to share a list of books that inspired and shaped me as well:

Create Your Best Year, One Day at A Time

by Clara Angelina Diaz

If Life is a Game, These are The Rules

by Cherie Carter-Scott

Practical Intuition

by Laura Day

The Power of Now

by Eckhart Tolle

A New Earth

by Eckhart Tolle

Way of the Peaceful Warrior

by Dan Millman

Ask and It's Given

by Esther and Jerry Hicks

When I'm processing feelings or when I have something I feel compelled to share, the first thing I do is pick up a pen and paper. I've found writing to lead me to inspired choices and it frees me from heavy feelings. There is so much healing that can be done by writing. I've often found sparks of inspiration or solutions to my problems just by writing them out. Writing, "Create Your Best Year, One Day at a Time" was like creating a guide for myself. It's a reminder that every day holds the potential to make the best days of my life, forever and always.

THE ADVICE

Looking back at my younger self, I would tell her: "Do everything in your power to become your own best friend mentally, physically, and spiritually. Many people can attempt to hurt, abandon, discount, and forget you, but you must not do that to yourself. Work on cultivating the voice of the wise and compassionate adult within."

For me, the biggest shift in my mindset was the practice of being 100 percent responsible for myself. From that place, I can receive more freely from others what they are willing to give. I no longer need to contort myself into any version of myself that I think they want me to be. I can own myself, my actions, and my decisions fully and completely.

For those of you who tend toward people-pleasing, this isn't an easy lesson to learn or an easy thing to practice. So many of us get uncomfortable when saying the word no or not conforming to meet other people's expectations. My advice is to practice. Practice saying no or being your authentic self and see what happens. It gets a little easier each time, I promise.

In that same vein, through a lot of therapy and practice, I have also learned to speak my true feelings despite fearing judgment. My goal is to be free and speak up, even when others choose to stay silent. Give yourself permission to have a voice and use that voice!

I also recommend creating practices that support you on a spiritual and emotional level. My favorite practices that I employ to support myself are meditation, contemplation, reflection, reframing, and asking for help early and often! Finding that inner stillness, thinking carefully about my actions and reactions, giving myself a break, detaching from a story that's holding me back, writing a new narrative, and enlisting a support team are all game changers in how I operate in the world.

When I think about the advice I would most want to impart to a young person trying to find their way, I would say it's important to be honest about what you need in all areas of your life. You are important, and you deserve love and support, just like any other human.

Decide what areas of your life you want to focus on and start pouring your energy there. You will be surprised by what grows from just giving attention to those areas of your life!

THE PATH FORWARD

You are powerful. You are so powerful that you create worlds and can co-create your reality. Get to know that power and get intimate with it! There are so many ways to do this! Spirituality, psychology, astrology, human design, therapy, mentoring, coaching and self-reflection have been my tools to know that I am a daughter of the Universe. Invest the necessary time to know yourself and live the highest version of who you are meant to be.

Educate yourself about yourself, the ways of this world, and the difference you want to make in it so that you can use your power effectively and responsibly. Do this to Lead and Liberate throughout your short trip on this earth?

You can be a co-creator of your life through a deep understanding and merging of who you are, who you want to be, and who you are called to become. Understanding yourself deeply will support you in becoming the leader you are meant to be.

ABOUT THE AUTHOR

A certified Master Coach for over 15 years, Clara Angelina Diaz-Anderson teaches Authentic and Executive Leadership Coaching at Harvard University School of Professional Development and Executive Education.

Clara is the founder of ClaraFying Coaching and Consulting Institute, a leadership development, executive coaching and consulting firm, where her team of coaches and consultants, lead culture transformation projects for a premier clientele that includes the City of Boston. Through culture assessments, analysis, and recommendations that include executive, career, and life coaching, DEIB consulting, organizational program creation, implementation and facilitation.

The institute also offers bilingual coaching, coaching certification training, leadership development courses, business advising, public speaking and custom-made workshops. As a multi-sector professional Clara has worked with historical local officials like the 1st Dominican Boston

City Councilor Julia Mejía and the first Capeverdean State Representative and State Senator Liz Miranda. Harvard Business School recruited Clara to teach, coach, facilitate, and monitor their inaugural Interpersonal Dynamic Lab for their 1st year MBA students. In addition to working with some of the best in their field, her dream is to contribute to building a world where love, dignity, equity and compassion are the norm and not the exception.

Clara is originally from the Dominican Republic, and identifies as afro-caribeña. Her mission is to help humanity awaken to their innate power. She is a published author of the book "Create Your Best Year One Day At A Time". She lives in a suburb of Massachusetts with her two children and husband.

Learn more and connect with Clara at:

Website: https://www.clarafying.com/

LinkedIn: https://www.linkedin.com/in/clarafying/

Email: clara.coaching.certification@gmail.com

GET THE TOOLS AND SUPPORT YOU
NEED TO **LEAD WITH CONFIDENCE**

BECOME A COACH

Empower your leaders as Professional Coaches (CPC)! Equip them to tackle challenges and drive growth.

GET COACHING

Grow your confidence and elevate every area of your life and work. Boosting self-assurance leads to greater success and fulfillment, transforming both personal and professional aspects.

RETREAT IN SAMANA

Leadership Wellness Retreat: Dec 5-9, Samaná, Dominican Republic.

START YOUR JOURNEY

Clarafying Coaching and Consulting is a leadership development firm founded by Clara Angelina Diaz-Anderson. We provide executive coaching and leadership development training to empower leaders and enhance organizational effectiveness.

ClaraFying
COACHING AND CONSULTING INSTITUTE

WWW.CLARAFYING.COM

Printed in Great Britain
by Amazon

55480821R00089